Please return this book to:
Mather Elementary School Library
24 Parish Street
Dorchester, MA 02122

my world of science

Simple Machines

Published in the United States of America by Cherry Lake Publishing
Ann Arbor, Michigan
www.cherrylakepublishing.com

Reading Adviser: Marla Conn MS, Ed., Literacy specialist, Read-Ability, Inc.
Content Adviser: Brittany Burchard M.Ed., Science teacher
Book Design: Jennifer Wahi
Illustrator: Jeff Bane

Photo Credits: ©eggeegg/Shutterstock, 5; ©wckiw/Thinkstock, 7; ©EKramar/Shutterstock, 9; ©PRESSLAB/Shutterstock, 11; ©Brocreative/Shutterstock, 13; ©Romrodphoto/Shutterstock, 15; ©Paradise on Earth/Shutterstock, 17; ©Grigvoven/Shutterstock, 19; ©Annette Shaff/Shutterstock, 21; ©Dmitry Kalinovsky/Shutterstock, 23, Cover, 8, 10, 18, Jeff Bane

Copyright ©2019 by Cherry Lake Publishing. All rights reserved. No part of this book may be reproduced or utilized in any form or by any means without written permission from the publisher.

Library of Congress Cataloging-in-Publication Data

Names: Marsico, Katie, 1980- author. | Bane, Jeff, 1957- illustrator.
Title: Simple machines / by Katie Marsico ; [illustrator Jeff Bane].
Description: Ann Arbor, Michigan : Cherry Lake Publishing, [2018] | Series: My world of science | Audience: K to grade 3. | Includes bibliographical references and index.
Identifiers: LCCN 2018003267| ISBN 9781534128927 (hardcover) | ISBN 9781534132122 (pbk.) | ISBN 9781534130623 (pdf) | ISBN 9781534133822 (hosted ebook)
Subjects: LCSH: Simple machines--Juvenile literature.
Classification: LCC TJ147 .M3354 2018 | DDC 621.8--dc23
LC record available at https://lccn.loc.gov/2018003267

Printed in the United States of America
Corporate Graphics

table of contents

Let's Study: Simple Machines.... 4

Glossary 24

Index 24

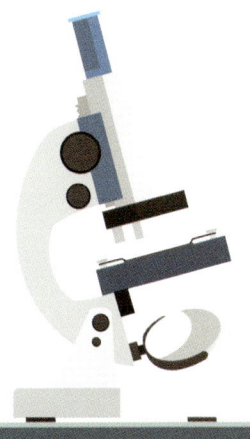

About the author: Katie Marsico is the author of more than 200 reference books for children and young adults. She lives with her husband and six children near Chicago, Illinois.

About the illustrator: Jeff Bane and his two business partners own a studio along the American River in Folsom, California, home of the 1849 Gold Rush. When Jeff's not sketching or illustrating for clients, he's either swimming or kayaking in the river to relax.

Let's Study: Simple Machines

Machines make work easier.

Some machines are really simple. You may be surprised!

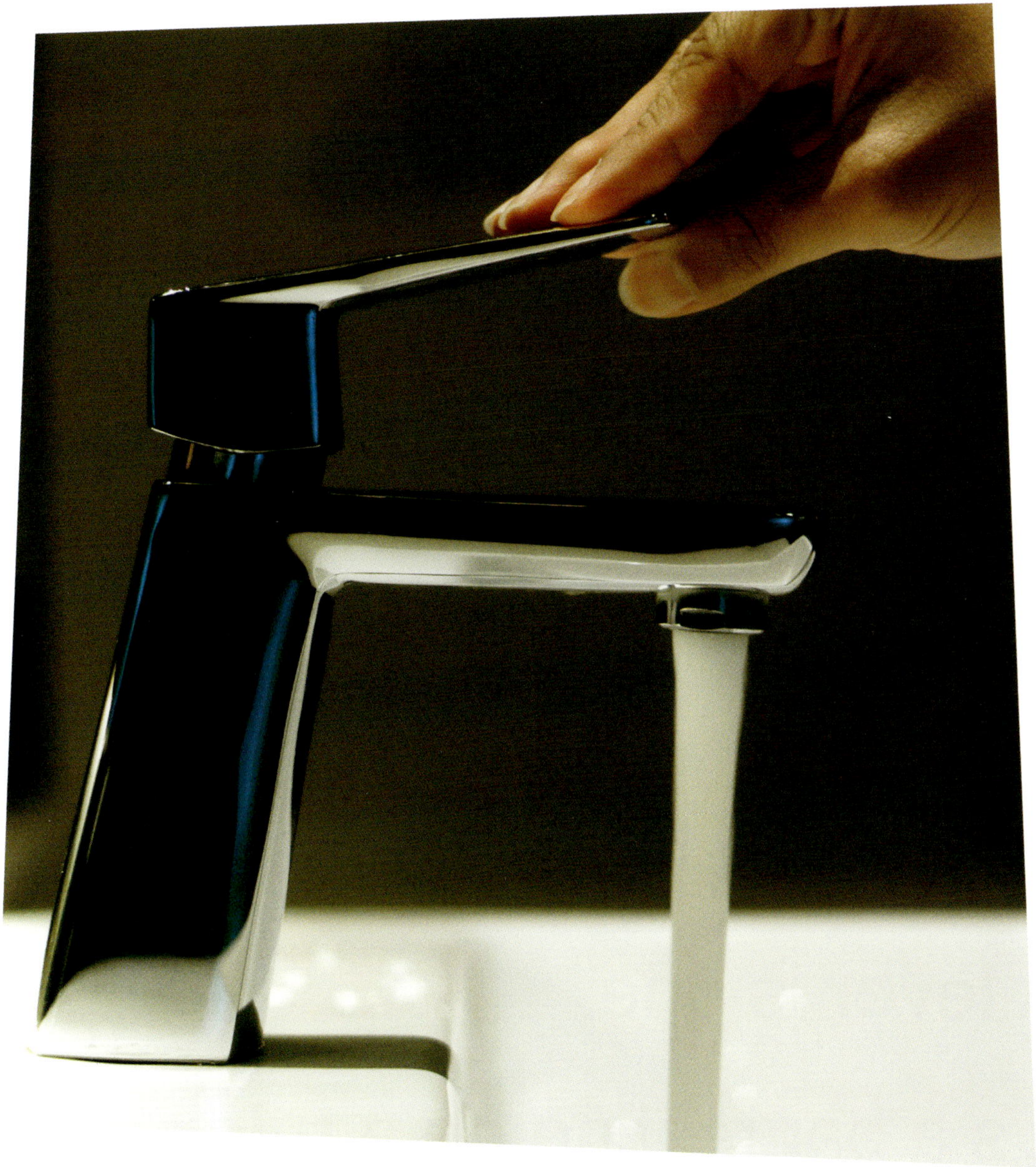

There are six simple machines.

A **lever** is one.

It's a bar resting on a **fulcrum**.

7

Levers can move heavy objects.

Seesaws are levers.

Scissors are a pair of levers.

What's another way a lever can help you?

A pulley is a simple machine.

It's a wheel with a rope around its rim.

Pulleys lift and lower objects.

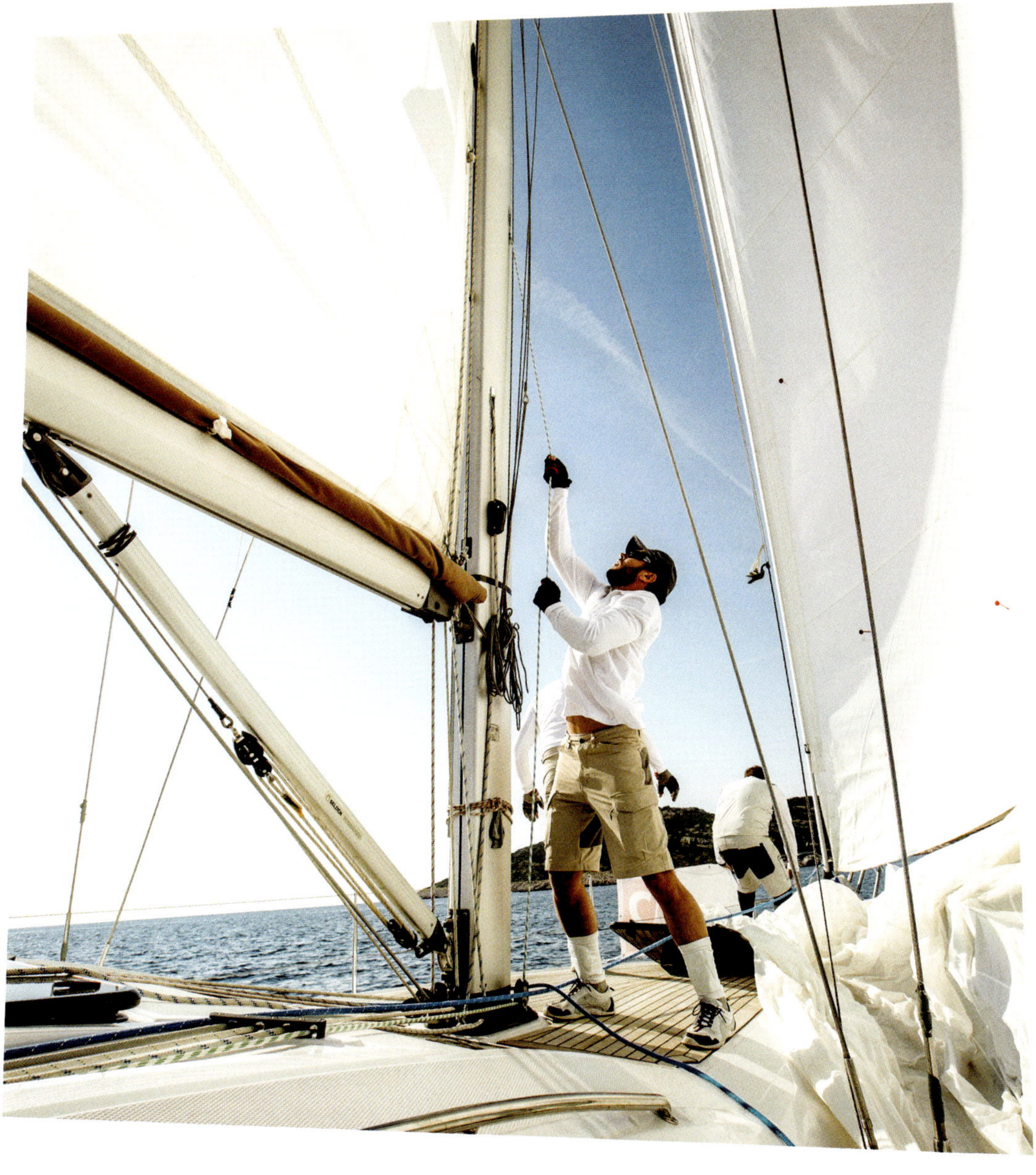

An inclined plane is a **ramp**.
A ramp is a simple machine.

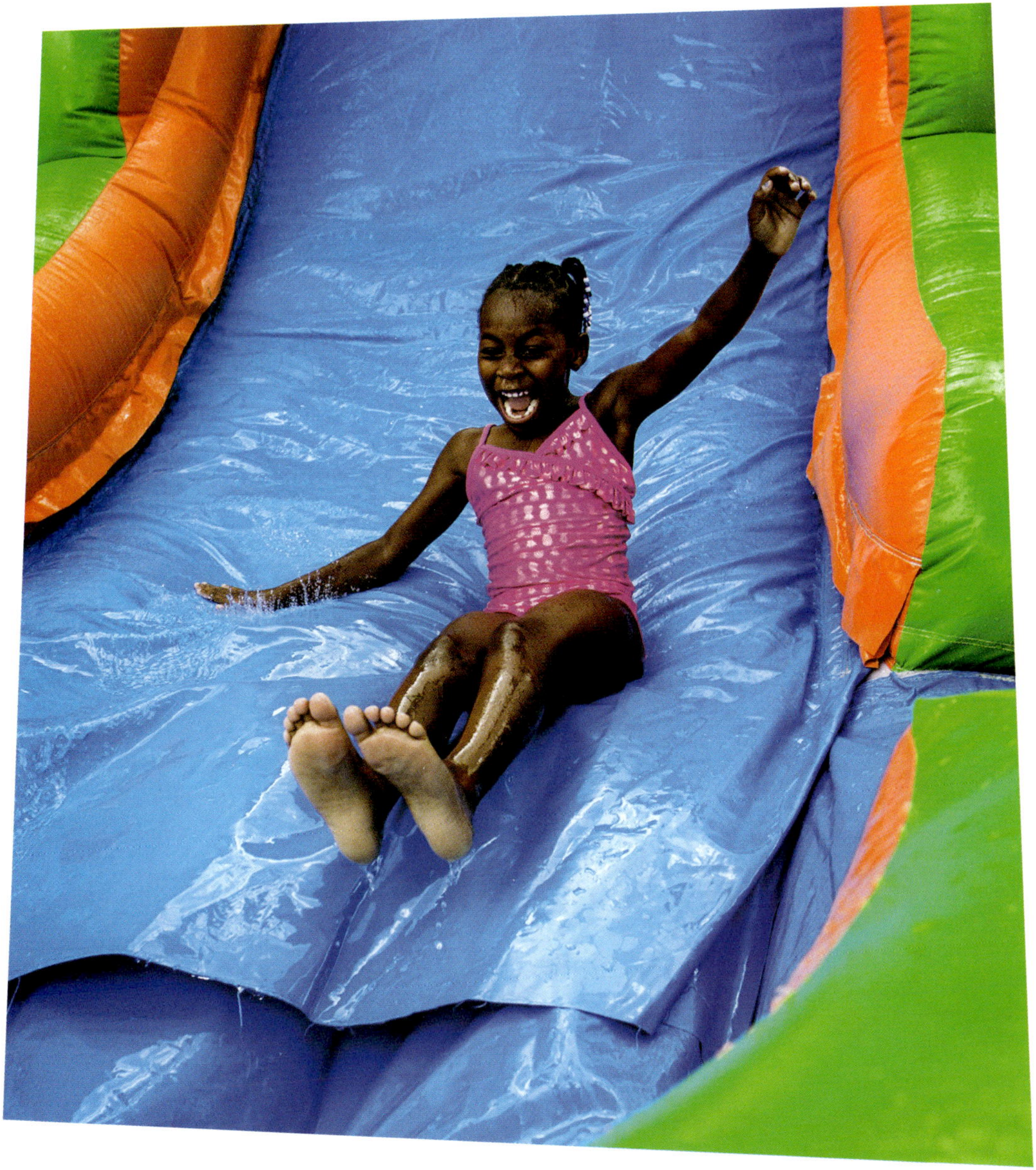

Picture a board. One end is higher than the other.

People move heavy things over inclined planes.

Can you find an inclined plane on your playground?

Wedges are simple machines.

One end of a wedge is thick.

The other is a thin point.

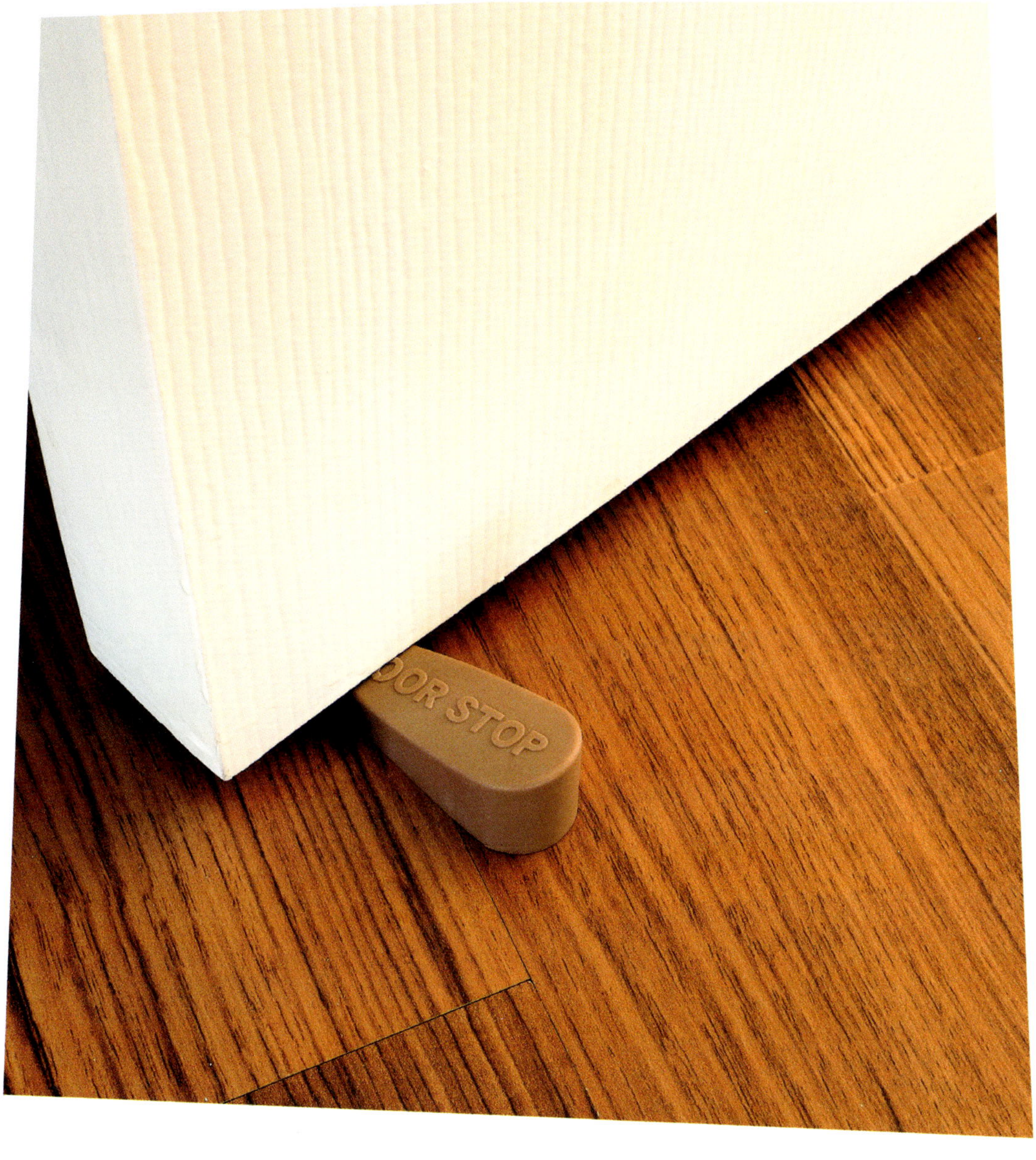
DOOR STOP

A screw is a simple machine.

Screws hold objects together.

One example is a jar lid.

What else is a screw?

A wheel and **axle** is a simple machine.

It is a wheel that spins on a rod.

That's how a door knob works!

21

Some **scientists** use simple machines. They ask questions. They look for answers.

What would you like to study next?

glossary & index

glossary

axle (AK-suhl) a pin that passes through the center of a wheel or group of wheels

fulcrum (FUL-kruhm) the point at which a lever balances its weight

lever (LEV-ur) a bar used to lift an object placed on one end by pushing down on the other end

ramp (RAMP) a slope that connects two different levels

scientists (SYE-uhn-tists) people who study nature and the world we live in

index

heavy, 8, 14

inclined plane, 12, 14

lever, 6, 8

machine, 4, 6, 10, 12, 16, 20, 22

pulley, 10

ramp, 12

screw, 20

wedge, 16

wheel, 10, 22